Don't Get Mad, Get Funny!

A light-hearted approach to stress management

Leigh Anne Jasheway

Illustrations by Geoffrey M. Welles

Pfeifer-Hamilton
Duluth, Minnesota

Whole Person Associates, Inc.
210 West Michigan
Duluth MN 55802-1908 218-727-0500

Don't Get Mad, Get Funny!

Printed in the United States of America
10 9 8 7 6 5 4 3 2

Editorial Director: Susan Gustafson
Art Director: Joy Morgan Dey
Manuscript Editor: Kathy DeArmond-Lundblad

Library of Congress Cataloging in Publication Data
96-60288

ISBN 1-57025-119-3

For my spouse, the good one, for only occasionally looking at me with THAT look when I refuse to take anything seriously, and for believing that laughter is almost as important as food (of course, he's tasted my cooking).

And of course, for my two wiener dogs, Copper and Slate, who are funnier than I'll ever be and who have taught me more about life than I have taught them about staying off the furniture.

Acknowledgments

According to my 50-lb. dictionary—which I use in lieu of a weight training program—"acknowledgment" means to admit or confess. Okay, so here we go. I confess that once in the third grade I stole a boy's GI Joe lunch box (my dad wouldn't buy me one). And then, from the eighth grade through grad school, I let people cheat off my tests. Not to mention . . .

Wait a minute. My editor has just informed me that what she really wants me to write in this section is a list of people I'd like to thank for their positive impact on me and my work. Well, why didn't you say so in the first place?

I'll try to make this brief because I know they'll start playing that Yanni music if I drone on too long . . .

Of course I wouldn't be here without my Mom (by the way, thanks Mom and sorry about those varicose veins!). Not only did she birth me, but she convinced me that a sense of humor could see you through almost any tragedy.

I'd like to thank Sam Cox and Paul Seaburn, my comedy coaches for first seeing in me the spark of humor and encouraging me to let it burn out of control. And for their continuing support and encouragement.

I owe a lot to Joel Goodman and The Humor Project, C.W. Metcalf, Patch Adams, and Steve Allen, Jr. (and many, many others) for paving the way for those of us who'd like to give the world a humor enema to relieve emotional constipation. And Molly Berger, a good friend, for showing me how to perform such a procedure.

Thanks to all the groups which have invited me in to

present Don't Get Mad, Get Funny workshops in the past five years. Especially those who had me present early in my career, before I actually knew what I was doing. There has been nothing more gratifying in my life than having people come up to me and say they plan to change their lives because of something I said—I only hope it wasn't the part where I suggested they go to work wearing fuzzy bunny slippers.

I owe a huge debt of gratitude to the people at Whole Person Associates, especially Susan Gustafson, for taking a chance on me. And you gotta give them credit for getting any work done at all, considering that ten months of the year, they're buried in a snowbank.

And, of course, I have to thank Dave Barry. If it weren't for his page-a-day calendars which I keep faithfully next to my computer, I may have sunk into unfunniness years ago.

Let's not forget my chiropractor and acupuncturist, the team of plumbers I have on retainer, my dogs' orthopedist, my high school guidance counselor who told me to consider a career in the actuarial sciences, my shrink, and anyone else who has ever listened to my jokes and had the kindness to humor me.

Well, that'll about do it. If I left you out and this makes you mad, just remember: DON'T GET MAD, GET FUNNY!

Table of Contents

Help!
I'm under so much
stress, my inner child
wants to be adopted!

Welcome to the overstressed majority! Our group is open to everyone; it doesn't matter whether you spend your time selling stock or selling shoes, raising kids or raising chickens, performing surgery or performing comedy. If you feel "stressed out," we're the support group for you!

These days, regardless of who you are or what you do, chances are that you feel like you spend most of your time racing the clock, worrying about things that may never happen, and feeling out of control. In fact, a recent Gallup Poll found that 40 percent of Americans feel stressed frequently, every day, and another 39 percent are sometimes stressed. If you're like me, on those rare occasions when you're not worrying about something, you worry about what it is that you've forgotten to worry about!

What is this crazy little thing called stress?

You'd expect that as members of the overstressed majority, we'd have a good handle on what stress is, right? Not necessarily. When most people talk about stress, they focus on unpleasant, and usually unexpected, things that happen every day—like being stuck on the freeway next to a car with music so loud it vibrates in your steering wheel,

being put on hold and having to listen to the polka version of the Beatles' greatest hits, or finding out this month's telephone bill is bigger than your paycheck. That's not stress. It's life.

There is a major difference between stressors—daily occurrences that have the potential for driving us crazy, or making us angry, frustrated, and hurt—and stress, the way we choose to respond to stressors. Let me repeat that last part—the way we *choose* to respond.

Although it doesn't feel like it, when you're late to a meeting because the dog swallowed your keys, you make a choice about how that situation will affect the rest of your day. You may beat yourself for being undependable, banish the dog to the backyard for a week, take out your hostility on everyone at work, or simply apologize for your tardiness by announcing, "A funny thing happened to me on the way to work . . . "

Throughout your day, whenever something unpleasant or unexpected happens, you make a choice how you will respond. The purpose of this book is to help you to see the "humor choice" and practice it every day.

What your body does when your mind says "Oh my God, not again!"

When faced with an unpleasant situation or stressor, your body undergoes a complicated series of events.

- The sympathetic nervous system sends messages throughout your body to "Prepare for Action!" Unfortunately, your body doesn't know whether it's preparing to change another wet diaper or to bolt out of the way of a moving train.

- The adrenal glands produce adrenaline and noradrenaline, a powerful combination. They increase your metabolism, dilate your blood vessels, increase your heart rate, and send extra glucose into your bloodstream to serve as a quick source of energy.

- Not to be outdone, the pituitary gland sends TTH and ACTH into the bloodstream. These guys speed up your metabolism, which sounds like a good thing if you've been trying to lose weight, but they also inhibit the production of sex hormones!

So, anyway, there you are, your hormones running amok, your heart pounding, your blood pressure rising, your energy level surging. Every part of your body is in a state of readiness to either fight the enemy or flee the scene. When the enemy, or stressor, is a 2-ton piano

hurtling towards your head, that's good. You need that extra burst of energy to sprint out of the way before you become a spot on the sidewalk. If, on the other hand, you are stuck in rush hour traffic, you can't fight (face it, you'd get beat up) or run away (unless you're willing to leave your car behind). You're all hyped up with no place to go!

Exercising your stress options

All of these physiological changes start the minute you perceive something as "negative"—whether it's a physical danger or simply a threat to your ego. Who among us hasn't felt the symptoms of stress when embarrassed in front of other people? It's pretty telling that the activity most Americans claim would cause them the most stress is speaking in public—a potential threat to their ego, not a physical threat.

To demonstrate just how automatic the classic stress response is, you may want to try this simple exercise:

- Grab a partner.

- Face each other and put your palms together.

- Have your partner push gently against your palms for three seconds.

Give it a try, then turn the page and find out how most people react when they are pushed—physically, mentally, or emotionally.

If you're like the average overstressed person, when your partner pushed, you pushed back, using the fight response. Or perhaps you were submissive and let yourself be pushed, using the flight response. Those are the typical responses to stress. And they just seem to happen.

If you stop and think about it, however, you could probably come up with dozens of alternatives to "push or be pushed." How about trying one of these options:

- Say "I don't have time for this nonsense!" and just drop your hands

- Tell a joke to make your partner laugh so hard he or she can't push anymore

- Tickle your partner into submission

- Leave the room and go out to rent a good movie

- Offer chocolate mousse as a bribe

- Twirl your partner into a polka

- Ask your partner to marry you

All of these are plausible responses, but they required some creative thinking. Our automatic reaction is to push back or submit. The trick is learning to *think* about stressors and to *choose* a response that helps you cope—a response that makes you feel calm, happy, in control, and happy.

Little stress
big stress

Major events like birth, death, marriage, and chronic illness take their toll on your body and mind. Anyone who has just had a new baby or gotten a divorce can vouch for that. But, fortunately for most of us, these major life events happen infrequently throughout our life. For instance, most of us only get married once or twice, unless you happen to be Zsa Zsa Gabor or Mickey Rooney.

Actually, though, it's the small, daily stuff that grinds us down, wears us out, and leaves us whimpering by the roadside. So, in reality, the small stuff is the big stuff when it comes to stress because it happens to us all the time— pots boil over on the stove, the dog pees on the new rug, the phone won't stop ringing, major appliances break down just when we need them the most—Aaargh!

The problem comes when you respond to every little annoyance with a full-blown stress response. Eventually, you'll use up all your "stress energy." This fighting and fleeing stuff is exhausting and overwhelming and can leave you feeling like a sponge that has been wrung out and left to dry. There's nothing left. And if a big stressor should then happen your way, you have so few re-sources remaining, the best you can do is pull the covers up and hide.

Unfortunately, when stuff is happening to you, it can be hard to decide whether it's little stuff or big stuff. The best way to sort it out each time you face a stressor, is to ask yourself the following questions:

1. Am I in physical danger? (Does it hurt now, will it hurt later?)

2. Is anyone I care about in danger?

3. Is there anything I can do right now to change the situation?

4. Will this situation have a long-term negative impact on my life?

5. Will getting mad help? (The answer to this one is always NO!)

If you answer "No" to the above questions, the stressor you are dealing with is moderate and you should try to find a humorous way to deal with it rather than wasting stress energy on it.

A quick note on humor and other stress management techniques

I believe that humor is the most effective and healthiest mechanism humans have available for coping with stress. But it's vital for you to use any and all means of reducing stress that work for you, including exercise, meditation, visualization, deep breathing, relaxation, turning off the TV, learning to say no, and so forth.

Combining proven stress management techniques with a humorous outlook on life won't make you stress-proof, but it will make you healthier, happier, and stronger!

Adding humor to traditional stress management techniques

- Visualize your mother-in-law . . . moving to another country.

- Breathe slowly and deeply . . . through a pig snout.

- Chant a joke mantra (A chicken goes into a bar . . . a chicken goes into a bar . . .).

- Practice relaxation techniques while wearing bunny slippers.

- Exercise vigorously by taking your pet ferret for a walk.

Positive ways to cope with being stuck in traffic

■ Write a funny poem about traffic jams.

■ Do inner thigh exercises with a tennis ball.

■ Imagine the life story of the person stuck in the car next to yours.

■ Sing along with the radio (make up your own lyrics).

■ Listen to your favorite comedian on tape.

■ Do facial exercises to prevent crows' feet.

■ Practice ways to ask your boss for a raise.

■ Flirt with another driver.

■ Check your oil.

■ Clean out your glove compartment.

Lessons you would have learned if you hadn't skipped this chapter

- Stress is not things that happen to you, it is how you *choose* to respond to things that happen to you.

- Wasting your stress energy on daily stressors will wear you out and run you down.

- Changing from your "automatic" stress response to one that is happier and healthier requires creative thinking and asking yourself questions about the things that make you feel stressed.

Last time I went to the doctor, the blood pressure cuff exploded

When you respond to every little stressor with the classic stress response, your nervous system, adrenal glands, and pituitary gland get bunched up like badly-fitting underwear! The toll this takes on your body and mind can be tremendous.

According to some researchers, up to 80 percent of all visits to doctors' offices are for illnesses and injuries associated with the stress response. The list of stress-related problems is enough to make you sick: accidental injuries, allergies, baldness, breathing difficulties, cirrhosis of the liver, headaches, heart disease, hypertension, impotence, incontinence, infertility, lung ailments, neckaches, psoriasis, rashes, stomach problems, ulcers, zits, and more. Stress also aggravates such problems as multiple sclerosis, diabetes, genital herpes, and even trench mouth.

It hurts when I get mad!

Trying to juggle too many priorities creates lots of stress. You really can't do it all and do it all perfectly. But if dropping a ball makes you feel angry at yourself and others, you're a candidate for a variety of stress-related problems.

Face it, when you get mad, you can feel your body tying itself in a knot, can't you? Whether that knot's in your stomach, your shoulders, your head, or your back doesn't matter. What matters is that the way you react to life's little unpleasantries may be the cause of many of your physical and mental health problems (or at least may be responsible for making them worse). You may want to take the test that follows to see how many of the classic signs of overstress you have.

Stress symptoms test

1. Which of the following best describes the amount of energy you have left at the end of the day?

    a. I could easily run a marathon.

    b. I have enough energy to enjoy my private and social life.

    c. I usually plop on the couch and stay there all night.

    d. I'm so tired, changing my underwear wears me out.

2. How would you describe your productivity level at work?

    a. I'm so productive, my in-box is empty.

    b. My in-box and my out-box are always about evenly divided.

    c. My in-box is buried somewhere under this mess

    d. I'd like to crawl in a box and hide.

3. How's your appetite?

    a. Healthy—I eat well and regularly.

    b. Okay—but, sometimes I skip meals when I'm busy.

    c. I'm usually either not hungry or starving—I can't seem to find a happy middle ground.

    d. Food? The thought of it makes me nauseous.

4. How tense are your muscles, especially those in your neck, shoulders, and back?

   a. Not at all tense.

   b. A little tense, but it goes away when I rest.

   c. I'm always in knots.

   d. I'm so stiff, my spouse uses me for an ironing board.

5. How well do you sleep?

   a. I fall asleep as soon as I go to bed and I sleep all night long.

   b. Occasionally I have trouble sleeping.

   c. I lie awake worrying and often wake up in the middle of the night.

   d. I've forgotten where the bedroom is.

6. How's your self esteem?

   a. I have high expectations of myself and I usually meet them.

   b. I'm mostly satisfied with myself.

   c. I never seem to do anything right.

   d. I stand out on the curb with a sign that says, "Will work for self esteem."

7. How often do you have fun?

   a. Every day—I make it a priority.

   b. At least once a week.

   c. Not very often—once a month or less.

   d. Never—I might get hurt!

If you answered "c" to more than half of the questions in the test on the previous two pages, you are displaying some of the classic symptoms of being under too much stress: lower energy, reduced productivity, loss of appetite, lack of motivation, difficulty sleeping, low self-esteem, and an inability to have fun. If you answered "d," you've also got some typical stress symptoms, but you seem willing to laugh about it, which is definitely a step in the right direction.

I'm my own worst enemy

When you're overstressed, sick, and your life appears to be going to the dogs, you have to do something. Unfortunately, many of us don't know how to appropriately respond, so we resort to "maladaptive" reactions to stress. "Maladaptive" reactions include drinking, drug use, smoking, overeating or undereating, angry outbursts, violence, addictive behavior (e.g., gambling, shopping, and exercise addiction), and risk-taking behavior.

When you respond to stress in any of these ways, you waste time and money on behaviors that are actually leaving you worse off and more miserable in the long run. What you need to do is finish this book quickly so you can get to work on managing your stress in ways that are healthier, happier, and certainly cheaper than a lot of things you may have been trying!

Lessons you would have learned if you hadn't skipped this chapter

- Too much stress makes you sick.

- Too much stress makes you a drag to be around.

- Too much stress makes you do stupid things to yourself and others.

Nyuk, nyuk, nyuk! What the three stooges knew about the benefits of humor

Just as you can feel the damage you're doing to your body when you respond negatively to a stressor, you know you feel good inside when you laugh. But rather than just a pleasant feeling, there's a whole bunch of things going on inside your body that cause that good feeling.

The diagram on the next page gives a good overview of some of the major physiological and psychological benefits of humor. No wonder you feel so good when you laugh! Your body is working like crazy for that feel-good feeling.

If you look closely at the diagram, you will notice that almost all the benefits of laughter counteract the negative

The Benefits of Laughter

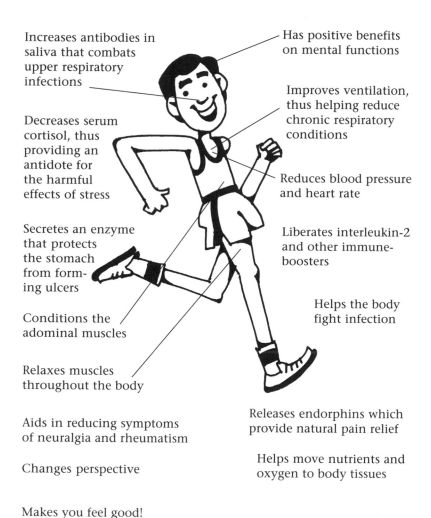

Increases antibodies in saliva that combats upper respiratory infections

Has positive benefits on mental functions

Improves ventilation, thus helping reduce chronic respiratory conditions

Decreases serum cortisol, thus providing an antidote for the harmful effects of stress

Reduces blood pressure and heart rate

Secretes an enzyme that protects the stomach from forming ulcers

Liberates interleukin-2 and other immune-boosters

Helps the body fight infection

Conditions the adominal muscles

Relaxes muscles throughout the body

Aids in reducing symptoms of neuralgia and rheumatism

Releases endorphins which provide natural pain relief

Changes perspective

Helps move nutrients and oxygen to body tissues

Makes you feel good!

physiological problems of the classic stress response. For example, while anger may give you a stomachache, laughter actually causes your body to secrete an enzyme that protects your stomach. Negative reactions to stress make your blood pressure go through the roof; after you laugh, your blood pressure and heart rate go down.

And rather than feeling bad all over like you do when you get angry, the endorphins produced by the body during laughter provide natural painkillers, so you actually feel better. These are the same hormones that produce euphoria that runners report, and you don't even have to run to get them. And, as long as you're avoiding running, you might as well cut out sit-ups, too. A good belly laugh is as much abdominal work as sit-ups—not to mention, a whole lot more fun. In fact, laughing provides exercise, and then relaxation, for muscles throughout the body, especially the muscles in the face!

Laughter also "massages" your internal organs. Besides feeling good , this massage can aid in digestion and improve the flow of blood and oxygen throughout the body. If you have a job where you sit down all day, a lot of your blood tends to settle in your hind quarters. For most of us, this is not the area of the anatomy we prefer to think from! One of the reasons many of us get a mid-afternoon slump is because there's too little oxygen going to our brain and too much going to our cellulite.

When you laugh, however, you get better blood flow

to all your major organs, including your brain. You can think more clearly, be more creative, and solve problems better. One study focused on people trying to solve a really complex puzzle. At the midway point, half the participants were sent out for coffee and the other half were sent out to watch "I Love Lucy" or other funny stuff. Those who had the comedy break solved the puzzle faster when they got back.

Additionally, because oxygen circulates more effectively, breathing improves, thus helping reduce symptoms of some chronic respiratory conditions. The symptoms of neuralgia and rheumatism also seem to be relieved by improved blood flow.

And, to top it off, preliminary studies also show that laughter may help combat upper respiratory infections by increasing production of an important antibody in the saliva, and laughter liberates interleukin-2 and other immune-boosters, thus strengthening the immune system. In the Resources section at the end of this book , you'll find a list of articles about how laughing affects physiology and emotions (for those of you who now feel an overwhelming desire to make sure I haven't lied to you about this stuff).

So, when you laugh, you actually are saving yourself from a life of pain, misery, and countless visits to the doctor!

Laughing is better than sitting on a cactus

Laughing is better than:

- Cutting yourself shaving

- Cleaning out the cat's litter box

- Biting your tongue

- Getting your nose pierced

- Sleeping funny and waking up with a crick in your neck

- Getting hit in the face by a slammed door

- Walking around in 4" spiked heels all day

- Wearing a thong leotard

- Holding your breath

MMMPPPPHHHH...

Laughter makes life easier

If you are willing and able to laugh at all life's little disasters, you will also find that other parts of your life will also become easier. That's because laughter (especially when you're laughing at yourself) does a lot of other important things, such as:

- It helps you communicate more effectively.

- It makes you more likeable.

- It helps people trust you.

- It makes you more fun to be around.

- People tend to be less threatened by you.

- It helps you develop perspective by removing you from your problems (and by putting more oxygen and blood in your brain).

- And, as Alan Alda said, "When people are laughing, they're generally not killing one another."

It's not funny!—moving from anger to laughter

Okay, so you agree that laughing is better for your mind, body, and soul than pounding your fist through the wall. But agreeing in principle doesn't really help when your boss is yelling at you and your blood pressure shoots up, and the funniest thing you think of starts with "@#$%^&&," and if you said that, you could get you fired!

In order to effectively use humor to cope with stress, you must do three things:

- understand your own humor and your ability and willingness to laugh;

- have a humor plan; and

- practice using your humor skills until they feel natural.

The next chapters provide you the tools for accomplishing the above three goals. So next time the you-know-what hits the fan and you'd really like to respond with a nice big smile or even a hearty laugh, YOU CAN!

Stress
and the U.S. mail

Once upon a time, my fiance and I went to the post office to mail our wedding invitations. It was Sunday, and the place was closed, except for the inside mail slot. I put the invitations into the slot one at a time, but quickly grew impatient. So I grabbed a whole handful and attempted to ram them into the slot. Although the invitations went in, my fingers would not come out!

One look at my fiance's face and I could tell he thought this was funny. One look at my face and he could tell that if he laughed, the wedding was off. Being the dutiful groom-to-be, he started pounding on the wall to alert someone to our premarital predicament.

Meanwhile, two other postal patrons came in to check their mailbox. Although they were perfectly polite while in the building, the minute they stepped outside, they burst out laughing.

I, on the other hand, was standing, fingers in slot, chanting my new mantra, "This is not funny! This is not funny!" Eventually a young man magically appeared from behind the wall with two screwdrivers. He pried me loose. I told him they should have a sign. "Do not put fingers in mail slot."

The situation was funny to everyone except me because they had perspective. What gave them perspective was that it wasn't happening to them! It could have been worse, I guess. I could have been in desperate need of a bathroom!

Lessons you would have learned if you hadn't skipped this chapter

- Laughter really is the best medicine.

- Laughter makes life easier.

- Using humor to manage stress requires that you understand yourself, make a humor plan, and practice using your humor skills until they feel natural.

Finding
your funnybone

Before you can begin to use humor as a stress management tool, you need to understand some things about your sense of humor and your ability and willingness to smile, giggle, or laugh so hard it hurts. Everyone has a different sense of humor and unless you are attuned to yours, you will end up missing many opportunities to use your humor skills to deal with life's little unexpected miseries.

A recent study reported that the average American five-year-old child laughs out loud around four hundred times a day, while the average adult laughs out loud only fifteen. Young children are truly hedonistic—when something is no longer fun, they stop doing it. We adults call that a short attention span.

Reaching adulthood does require a degree of buckling down and getting serious. Let's face it—there are things we have to do whether we want to or not. But so many of us have lost the sheer capacity for fun, joy, and laughter that even when we have the opportunity, we miss it.

Many adults face a debilitating disease that has never been medically diagnosed: humor impairment. Humor impairment is the inability to find humor even in situations that are funny to most other people. My personal term for this state is constipation, because if you can't release your emotions through laughter, your emotional and spiritual systems are "backed up."

Your level of humor constipation is often a result of the environment in which you grew up. If laughter was always present in your family, your ability and willingness to laugh with others is probably great. On the other hand, if, like myself, you grew up in a family where laughter was frowned upon, you will probably find it more difficult to express humor in front of others.

But, as with any other behavior, you can change. I grew up in a family where expressing any type of emotion was seen as a sign of immaturity. As a result, I was a most serious child, preferring Edgar Allen Poe and Sylvia Plath to the daily comics. I married a man who believed that neither laughter nor tears were acceptable or desirable. Today, however, I make my living teaching laughter and comedy and performing as a stand-up comic. My background has truly taught me how bleak and unhealthy a life without humor can be. (By the way, I still love Edgar Allen Poe and Sylvia Plath, but now they rub shoulders on my bookshelves with books by Dave Barry and Rita Rudner.)

The rest of this chapter consists of exercises for you to do to get a better sense of your sense of humor. Be sure to try them out.

Your laughter profile

Take this short quiz to determine how willing and able you are to laugh at life and its foibles.

1. During an average day, I laugh out loud, snicker or giggle:

    a. Once or not at all

    b. Two or three times

    c. At least once an hour

    d. Constantly, I'm under medication

2. When I am alone and read, see, hear, or think something funny, I:

    a. Smile to myself

    b. Laugh out loud, but look around to see if anyone saw me

    c. Laugh out loud and find someone with whom to share the funny thing

    d. Take a cold shower

3. In the past year, I can remember:

    a. At least one time I spent at least a whole minute laughing

    b. At least two to five times I spent at least a whole minute laughing

    c. More than five times I spent at least a whole minute laughing

    d. I can't remember—what was the question?

4. When I'm around other people, they laugh and joke:

    a. Never

    b. Sometimes

    c. Often

    d. I never hang around other people, they might laugh at me!

5. When faced with daily crisis (the dog peed on the rug, I missed the project deadline again, my daughter needs brownies for school NOW!), I respond with a laugh:

    a. Never

    b. Sometimes

    c. Often

    d. Only if it's someone else's rug, deadline, or child

6. I do things intentionally to make myself laugh

    a. Never

    b. Sometimes

    c. Often

    d. That might hurt!

7. The people I spend most of my time with:

    a. Leave me feeling drained and depressed

    b. Don't really affect my attitude

    c. Make me laugh a lot

    d. Usually steal my lunch money

8. I can name:

   a. One thing that almost always makes me laugh

   b. Two things that almost always make me laugh

   c. At least three things that almost always makes me laugh

   d. My closest relatives

9. I laugh at myself:

   a. Never

   b. Sometimes

   c. Often

   d. Only when I'm not in the room

10. I do silly things on purpose (wear strange buttons, make funny noises, and do things to see how others will respond):

   a. Never

   b. Sometimes

   c. Often

   d. No one ever notices

11. When I hear people laughing at work, the first thing I think is:

   a. I wish I could get paid to goof off

   b. I wish I knew what the joke is

   c. How wonderful that they're having a good time, I think I'll join them

   d. That it's Saturday and I shouldn't even be here

How to score
your laughter profile

Give yourself the following points for each letter:
a=0 b=1 c=2 d=3. Then add them up to obtain your total score.

If your score is less than 5, you are suffering from humor malnutrition. Someone probably told you "Grow up, get serious!" and you did. In order for you to find the humor in daily events, you will have to start slowly—first by convincing yourself that humor is a acceptable emotion and one that is healthy when used regularly.

If your score is from 6 to 15, you occasionally have a good laugh, but your life lacks humor regularity. Remember, laughter is like exercise—you have to do it regularly to get the full benefit. Use it or lose it! You're good at expressing humor when you find things funny, but your goal now is to try to find humor in those things that usually make you angry, annoyed, or irritated.

If your score is from 16 to 20, you are humorously fit! Not only do you approach life with the right amount of humor and benefit from it, you also probably make other people's lives more enjoyable. You should become a friend and role model for people around you who need the healing power of humor yet who don't seem to be able to use it in their lives.

If your score is from 21 to 33, you're downright silly, aren't you? Don't stifle those childish instincts! Sure they told you in school that the class clown would never go anywhere in life. But they were wrong! Look at Robin Williams! He's taking it to the bank!

But whatever you do, don't get mad about your score on the laughter profile. In the following chapters, you'll learn how to raise it.

Your humor compass: where do you find the funny in life?

Now that you have a better idea of your ability and willingness to use humor on a daily basis, it is important to understand the kinds of things that you find funny. After all, just as our taste in food or art varies, so does our taste in what is and is not funny to us.

An important note here: You do not necessarily have to laugh out loud to find something funny. One of my best friends and I went to a movie together a few years ago. I laughed so hard I couldn't see through the tears. She sat there quietly. Afterwards, she said the movie was one of the funniest she had seen in years.

Ask yourself the following questions to determine the types of humor that you will be able to use to most effectively manage your stress:

- Do you laugh more at the physical or slapstick humor you find in *The Three Stooges*, *I Love Lucy*, *Perfect Strangers*, and *The Mask*, or do you prefer verbal humor, or do you enjoy both?

- Do you have a strong sense of humor ethics? In other words, do you find certain specific types of jokes to be offensive rather than funny?

  It is important for you to understand the types of humor that distress you rather than tickle you.

They may include stereotypical jokes, put-downs, or humor about certain subjects that are too close to your heart for you to find them funny at present.

■ Do you like jokes that focus on things you have in common with the comedian?

Studies indicate that many people do prefer humor that speaks to their own personal experience, which means that we often prefer comedy from people who are similar in age, race, or gender.

■ Do you like topical humor, jokes that build on current events?

Late night humorists are scheduled to appear on television after the news to help people cope with the negative images painted during the evening newscast. If this type of humor is appealing to you, you can try, yourself, to find humor in your local newspaper and nightly news reports.

- Do you like wordplay and puns?

  An interesting thing that I have discovered is that different types of humor appear to be more or less popular in different parts of the United States. When teaching humor classes, I have noted, for example, that people from the Midwest tend to enjoy the humor of puns more than people from other areas of the country.

- Do you prefer humor that stands on its own, or do you like props and gimmicks?

  Some people find Gallagher extremely funny (for those of you who don't know, he's the guy famous for smashing watermelons on stage). Others think he's just silly.

- Do you regularly find humor in things that aren't necessarily meant to be funny?

  For example, do you make jokes about commercials, billboards, medical forms, or warning labels on food packages?

Answering these questions for yourself will help you identify the types of humor to seek out, as well as the types of humor you yourself may attempt in order to reduce your stress and have more fun in life.

Your misery index

At some point after a moderately stressful event, most of us will find some humor in our own predicaments. As Steve Allen, Jr. says, "Comedy equals tragedy plus time." The length of time between when the stressor occurs and when you find it funny is your misery index.

Let's take an example. Suppose you've just discovered that the drycleaner has ruined one of your favorite items of clothing, one that you planned to wear this evening to a special event. How long do you estimate it will take before you are able to find any humor in the situation— a day? A week? A month? A year? This is the amount of time you choose to be miserable. Many people choose never to let go of petty situations.

Most of us don't really know how much misery we choose for ourselves. The exercise that follows requires that you start paying attention to your responses to moderate stressors during the next week. Use the form on the next page to evaluate your misery index.

My misery index			
Stressor	Date	Date I laughed	How I found the humor

Here's an example of my table might look filled in at the end of a week:

My misery index			
Stressor	Date	Date I laughed	How I found the humor
Drycleaners ruined shirt	2/16/96	2/18/96	Told friend about it, and she told me a funny drycleaning story
Found scratch on new car	2/17/96	2/23/96	Just decided to laugh because I didn't like feeling miserable
Phone rings in middle of night with wrong number	2/17/96	2/17/96	Even though sleepy, joked around with person on other end
Hurt back digging in garden	2/18/96	2/19/96	Watched Roseanne— episode was about her bad back—made me laugh
Insurance company rejected claim for eye appointment last month	2/20/96		Still working on it

For many people, the time between the stressor and the humor will be much longer than a week. Keep track of your stressors for one week, but continue to track your responses until you actually find some humor in each situation.

Completing this grid will give you a good idea of how long you choose to be miserable. It will also allow you to set goals for yourself. If, for example, it takes you on average of two weeks to find humor in moderately stressful events, you could set a goal to cut that amount of misery in half! The tools in the next chapters will show you how.

What you would have learned if you hadn't skipped this chapter

- How willing and able you are to laugh at life

- What kinds of things make you laugh, snicker, giggle, or guffaw

- How long you hold on to misery before letting loose with humor

Procrastination can be hazardous to your health!

Once, I was scheduled to do a presentation for five hundred emergency room nurses. Unfortunately, I waited until the last day before making my handouts or sorting through my slides. Can you spell P-R-O-C-R-A-S-T-I-N-A-T-I-O-N?

I copied my handouts and went to the AV department to borrow their slide-sorting tray. They asked me to be very careful because it was the only one they had (at this point, the theme music from *Jaws* should have begun to play!).

Because the tray wouldn't stay open, I propped it up with my glass of water. During a phone call, I noticed a strange smell coming from my desk. I turned around and found that my glass of water had tumbled over and that a small fire was blazing. The slide-sorting tray had combusted and all my slides were melting to my desk.

Ever quick to action, I put out the fire with my soggy handouts. I returned the tray, totally destroyed to the AV department and said, "You want to hear a funny story?" During the presentation the next day, I made references like, "The next slide, were it not melted to my desk, would illustrate this point."

That's a plan, Stan!

Now that you understand more about your sense of humor and how well you use it, you're ready to formulate a plan to deal with your daily stressors. This chapter will help you do two things:

- Evaluate the types of regular occurrences in life that typically cause you to react with the fight or flight stress response; and

- Determine the types of things that you find humor in. Problem—solution!

The only way a plan works, however, is if you actually use it. The best thing to do once you have made the two lists suggested in this chapter is to put them where you can see them every day—on the wall near your desk, on your refrigerator door, on a note pinned to your lapel, if need be!

Regular stressor list

This task is simple, but important. You need to make a list of all the things that occur with regularity in your life that almost always set off your stress response. This list may even include the names of people who annoy you all the time. But be careful and don't let them see the list!

Creating this list should take about one month. Continue to add things as they occur, however. For example, mechanical equipment breaking down may be high on your list, but because it may not happen during the month you're developing your list, you may forget it. Add it when you think of it.

Your list should be as specific as possible. It is not enough to say your job causes you to feel stress. You should try to determine whether it's the people you work with, office politics, poor environmental conditions, low pay, too much work, too little or too much supervision, your specific tasks, or a feeling of lack of progress that's really to blame for your feelings.

In order to get as much detail as possible in your list, be sure to include any of the following:

- People (specific people who drive you crazy, or types such as plumbers or politicians)

- Personality quirks (rudeness, know-it-allness, unreliability)

- Habits (channel changing, leaving the cap off the toothpaste, cleaning ear with underwear)

- Things (potholes or empty gas tanks)

- Situations (being stuck in traffic or late for work)

- Tasks (unloading the dishwasher, resetting the VCR, calling your parents, etc.)

- Events (fireworks, large gatherings of people, family reunions, etc.)

- Environmental factors (heat, noise, light)

- Ideas (conservatism, liberalism, etc.)

- Others (be creative)

Begin your list by making several photocopies of the worksheet on the following page. Keep one at home, one in the car, and one at your workplace.

Remember, be specific. Focus on things that regularly happen in your life. And keep your list targeted at those things that typically make you react negatively.

To help you get started, here are some of the things that are at the top of my list.

- Being put on hold for more than 3 minutes at a time

My regular stressors

List everything that makes you feel angry, frustrated, annoyed, or hostile.

- Waiting in long lines that don't seem to move

- Voice mail systems in which I can never reach a real human being

- Loud noises (hammering, sawing, heavy metal, rap music, car alarms)

- Repair people who never arrive and never call

- Unexpected projects at work that suddenly were due yesterday

- Service people who don't want to help

- Drunks

- Dealing with insurance companies

- Having to fix things

- My husband zapping through all the TV channels with the remote control

- Being wakened out of a sound sleep by something unimportant

- Injuries or illnesses of any kind

- People who never let me get a word in edgewise (this takes real talent on their part)

- Arguing with someone over something stupid

- The gas tank on empty

- Day after day of hot weather

- Being treated like I'm stupid

- People who don't listen when I talk, forcing me to repeat myself

- Watching the television news

- Wondering where my money goes

Well, that's the short list anyway. What I have done is written down everything I can think of that used to make me angry, frustrated, annoyed, or hostile. Of course, they don't anymore because I use humor as a weapon! More about that later.

You can put your list in priority order (what stresses you the most or what happens most often), alphabetical order, or the order it occurs to you. The important thing is to actually do the exercise so you will have a good idea of the types of things you need to combat with humor.

Happiness list

When you're happy, you usually laugh—or, if you're currently humor-impaired, you may smile, giggle, or just relax that furrowed brow for a few seconds. A happiness list may include some things that are proven laughgetters (comedians, funny TV shows, comics, etc.), but should not be limited to those. Anything that makes you happy has value as a humor tool.

A good way to start this list is to try to remember what made you happy when you were a young child (remember, children are out there laughing all the time!). You can still enjoy many of the things you loved as a child, whether it's swinging in the park, building sandcastles on the beach, blowing bubbles, hula-hooping, or whatever.

The jury's still out on this one

I got called for jury impanelment a few years ago. That's where you sit in a big room with hundreds of other people on hard wooden seats waiting to see if they'll call your name so you can have the distinct pleasure of spending countless days with unwashed strangers arguing over the fate of someone's life while you eat bad deli food and remember fondly that stack of work you could be doing at the office. Since waiting is on my list of things that tick me off, I prepared in advance by taking a copy of one of my favorite Dave Barry books with me.

For six hours, I sat and read and laughed out loud like a hyena. I did not get picked for jury duty. I am fairly certain they thought I was insane!

Learning what you enjoyed as a child also helps you tap into adult happiness tools. For example, if your favorite childhood activities were primarily physical (climbing trees, building forts, or riding a bike, for example), you may find that as an adult, it is the physical activities that still provide you the most happiness. On the other hand, if you preferred mental activities—playing pretend, finger-painting, or dressing up—you may find that mentally-challenging activities bring you the most enjoyment.

Be sure to include on your list anything that makes you feel happy and that does not hurt you in the long run.

Again, to help you start to think about your list, here are some items from my personal list:

- My husband (when he's not zapping the remote control)

- My wiener dogs!!!

- Making up songs about my wiener dogs

- Full-body massages

- Bubble baths

- Making other people happy

- Listening to good music

- Exercise

- Being outdoors in nature

- Playing with Silly Putty

- Coloring

- Blowing bubbles

- Comedy (watching it and doing it)

- Singing

- Writing

- Playing my guitar

- Talking with happy friends

- Working

- Cheesecake

- Taking pictures

All of these things don't always make me happy, but there's always something on the list, that no matter my mood or situation, is guaranteed to make me feel better! You will notice that a lot of the things on my list are childlike. I assure you I have been known to walk down the halls at work blowing bubbles when I needed help coping with something in my life!

Your objective is to create a list for yourself of things that make you happy. Again, be as specific as you can. Make several photocopies of the worksheet on the next page so you'll always have one handy. Give yourself at least one month to develop this list so that you will be able to identify as many humor tools as possible.

My happiness list

List everything that makes you feel happy and does not hurt you.

Your humor plan

If you've spent the past month developing your two lists, you have your humor plan in hand. It's as simple as using your happiness tools to deal with your regular stressors.

For example, perhaps loud noises really stress you out. And, perhaps, your son's heavy metal band meets in your garage one Thursday every month and for some reason you have to be home. Knowing that the stressor is coming and knowing that, let's say, watching *M*A*S*H* always makes you laugh, you have all the tools you need for coping with stress with humor before it actually happens! (Also, be sure, in this case, to invest in a good set of earplugs!)

Now, wasn't that easy?

Things you would have learned if you hadn't skipped this chapter

- It is important for you to know exactly what types of things cause you to react with the classical stress response

- Making a list of things that make you happy can be as easy as A-B-C

- Problem—Solution—Voila! You have a plan!

Humor and home repair

Neither my husband nor I are any good at home repair. If left to fix something by myself, I'm usually okay, because I'll give it five minutes and then I'll call a professional (really empowered women do that!). My husband, on the other hand, thinks he can fix anything with duct tape, bubble gum, or a nice flat rock.

Putting us together to make minor home repairs is just asking for it. Let's say we have to install drapery hardware. Somewhere between finding the instruction sheet and losing the first screw, I will inevitably end up muttering, "You're a man, you should know how to use a screwdriver!" And he will end up responding, "You're

a feminist, you shouldn't expect me to know how to use a screwdriver!"

Because we know this is going to happen, we use our humor plan. We choose something from our list of things that make's us laugh and do it together before we ever embark on adventures in home destruction. We do something as stupid and simple as changing the lyrics to a favorite song to include the words "wiener dogs" ("And she's riding a wiener dog to Heaven") or quoting scenes from one of our favorite funny movies ("Inconceivable!"—a line from *The Princess Bride*). By laughing together, we become more willing to work together, and our bodies help protect us from the damage of the stressor we know is coming.

We also apologize beforehand. Hey, it's easier to say "I'm sorry" when you are actually still talking to someone!

Your humor tools: simple steps

The key to using humor to deal effectively with your stress is to put more humor in your life. If you are surrounded by things that regularly make you laugh, it becomes easier and more natural to laugh at all life's little stressors.

This chapter focuses on the easiest ways you can begin to add more humor to your life. I recommend you do all or most of these steps before moving on to the more difficult—but also very rewarding—steps outlined in the following chapter.

Make funny friends

The quickest and easiest way to inject more humor into your life is to surround yourself with people who make you laugh. You don't have to be funny yourself; you just have to be astute enough to tell the difference between someone who always leaves you in stitches and someone who makes you want to call the Crisis Hotline!

Here are some easy steps for making sure there are plenty of people in your social circle who make you laugh:

- Identify the people in your life who use humor often and well.

- Maintain regular contact with those people—call, visit, write, e-mail, or use whatever form of communication is available and appropriate.

- Cultivate a humor buddy. Choose one person in your life to work with on expanding your humor horizons. On a regular basis (once a month at least), go see funny movies, write funny letters, tell jokes, send funny gifts. Your humor buddy may well be your spouse. In fact, research indicates that a shared sense of humor is one of the strongest predictors of the long-term success of a marriage.

- When you feel overstressed, make sure that you include one or more funny friends among those from whom you seek advice and solace.

- When making friends, seek out people who make you laugh and who share a similar sense of humor.

- If you have a friend who everyone says should be a stand-up comic, attempt to learn how he or she finds humor in daily life.

- Try to be a funny friend yourself.

Spend your money on funny

Thing that make you laugh are everywhere. Once you've found your sense of humor, a quick scout around will turn up all sorts of stuff that should tickle your newly-exposed funny bone. Here's a quick sampling:

- Animal snouts (from pig snouts to duck bills to lobster claws)

- Books (anything you find funny, whether it was meant to be or not)

- Buttons ("Stop me please before I become my mother!")

- Calendars (cartoons, features from your favorite humor author, funny pictures)

- Cards (there's no occasion that does not have a humorous card option)

- Coffee mugs (I like the kind with the surprise in the bottom of the mug)

- Doormats ("Warning: These Premises Patrolled By Guard Hamster!")

- Drinking straws (featuring dinosaurs, unicorns, penguins, and odd creatures not of this world)

- Furniture (how about barstools painted like cows with udders below?)

- Koozies ("Support Mental Health: Go Crazy")

- Music (one of my personal favorite groups for talent and humor is Trout Fishing in America)

- Pens and pencils (with funny sayings or creatures on top of them)

- Pictures and posters (anything you find funny)

- Post-it notes ("You don't have to be crazy to work here . . . we can train you.")

- Shoelace grabbers (all kinds of cartoon characters can grab your laces)

- Telephones (from Garfield to ducks that go quack in the night)

- Ties (from plain ugly to the Three Stooges)

- T-shirts (if it's been said, it's on a T-shirt)

- Troll dolls (featuring your favorite activity)

- Underwear (with chili peppers or lobsters or Disney characters)

By regularly purchasing things that make you laugh, you will surround yourself with humor and make laughter more easily accessible. My computer room, because it is so often stressful, is decorated in troll dolls and stuffed animals.

A quick browse through the yellow pages for your town may help you turn up a favorite spot to search for funny products. You may also want to check out catalogs that are listed in the Resources section at the end of this book.

Celebrating with humor

Celebrations offer great opportunities for fun and frivolity. Unfortunately, as adults, many of us get trapped by unrealistic expectations, perfectionism, and other beasts that prevent us from enjoying holidays and other special events.

Here are some easy steps you can take to add humor to your celebratory events:

- Invite a funny friend or a professional comic to write material for the special guest.

- Hold celebrations in locations where humor is part of the ambience. Instead of going to a stuffy restaurant for a family celebration, take everyone out to sing karaoke or to see a funny movie instead. This is a great idea when you have family members over during the holidays and the stress is getting so thick, you can cut it like fruitcake.

- Send funny invitations and thank you notes.

- Celebrate with a theme. Invite guests to come as their favorite comedian or cartoon character or bring a funny gifts. Select music that is fun and funny, for example, Ray Stevens, Weird Al Yankovic, Julie Brown, Trout Fishing in America, Peter Alsop . . .

- Integrate humor into regular meetings of friends or family. Play funny games like Balderdash, Twister or Tabloid Teasers. Encourage everyone to tell a funny story. Take pictures.

- Celebrate unusual holidays like Accordian Awareness Month, Bad Poetry Day, or No Socks Day (all of these are actual holidays). You can get information on unusual and fun holidays by referring to

Chase's Calendar of Annual Events at the reference desk of your local library.

Create your own humor library

Having your favorite humor resources readily at hand will make it easier to choose humor to cope with a hectic day or a stressful week . . . month . . . year . . . life . . . Begin now to start your library.

- Books—Really funny books are easy to find and are often available secondhand at local used bookstores. Once you've identified the types of humor that are most effective at tickling your funny bone, it's easy to stock your own personal library. Be sure to include humor books, books by your favorite cartoonists, and screenplays of your favorite funny movies or TV shows.

  Some of my personal favorite authors are Dave Barry, Jerry Seinfeld, Paul Reiser, Woody Allen, Rita Rudner, James Callahan, Andy Rooney, Bill Cosby, Berke Breathed, Gary Larson, Charles Schulz, Bruce Feirstein, and Jan King. I also have scripts from *Mad About You* and *Northern Exposure* in my library. Scripts are available from ScriptCity, 1-800-676-2522.

Quotes about humor

Fear is the lock and laughter is the key to your heart.

Crosby, Stills, and Nash

What the people need is a way to make them smile.

Doobie Brothers

It's never too late to have a happy childhood.

Tom Robbins

A man is about as happy as he makes up his mind to be.

Abraham Lincoln

Laughter is the shortest distance between two people.

Anonymous

Comedy equals tragedy plus time.

Steve Allen, Jr.

Most of the time, I don't have much fun. The rest of the time, I have no fun at all.

Woody Allen

Let's all be abnormal and act like ourselves.

Peter Alsop

We laugh to keep sane.

Peter Alsop

Those who shun the whimsy of things will experience rigor mortis before death.

Tom Robbins

Pain is inevitable, suffering is optional.

Anonymous

We can never really love anybody with whom we never laugh.

Agnes Repplier

ASAP means As Silly As Possible.

Alan Black

Humor is the instinct for taking pain playfully.

Max Eastman

Whatever *we* think is funny *is* funny.

Steve Allen, Jr.

The more I get to thinking, the less I tend to laugh.

Paul Simon

You grow up the day you have your first real laugh, at yourself.

Ethel Barrymore

Don't get your knickers in a knot. Nothing is solved, and it just makes you walk funny.

Kathryn Carpenter

- Movies—You should have a list of your favorite funny movies so you can easily select videos to rent when you need a comic break. I also recommend that you own at least one favorite funny movie on videotape so you can pull it out and watch it in an emergency.

  A good way to develop a personal list of funny movies is to check out a guide to movies on video from your local library. Jot down any you've seen that made you laugh plus those that you've been wanting to see.

- TV programs—No, CNN does not count as humor! If you have time for television at all, select educational programs and those that are emotionally and physically healing. Television can help you reduce stress if you use it with wisdom and humor.

- Clipped articles—Any time anything makes you laugh out loud, you should save it in a humor file. Your local newspaper is probably the source of lots of humor, and not only in the funnies. One of my favorites is a headline from a medical columnist entitled "Overuse of enemas can cause big trouble." It wasn't meant to be funny, but it cracked me up.

If you put all these together, you'll have a great humor library, full of examples of how to find the funny in life.

Communicate with humor

We all communicate constantly, whether in writing, speaking, or the way we dress and act. Humor is one of the most effective ways of getting a message across, and at the same time, it provides stress relief for both the sender and the receiver.

If you have to put something in writing—whether it's a letter home, a grocery list, or a memo to the cafeteria about the cockroach you found in your meatless lasagna, you can easily make it humorous. Try any of the following:

- Put your message on something humorous like a card, postcard, funny post-it note, toilet paper, or sweat socks.

- Include a funny quote.

- Include a cartoon.

- Include a really ugly picture of yourself, like your driver's license picture.

- Put a humorous sticker on it. I affix Mr. Yuk stickers to my bills.

- Have it delivered in an unusual manner—hidden in a fortune cookie, peeking out of a bellydancer's costume, or carried proudly by a Saint Bernard.

Also, think about adding humor to some of the other ways you may regularly communicate with others, such as:

- Telephone answering machine message

- E-mail

- Bulletin board

And, last but not least, there's verbal communication. To add humor to your life when communicating in person, you can include any of the suggestions for written communication (such as funny lines from movies) in your daily conversations. Try to remember cartoons, funny quotes, funny pictures and relay them to the people in your life. You do not have to be funny yourself or be able to remember a joke to make people laugh!

Storytelling

All of us have a funny stories to tell. Unfortunately, as Americans, we don't put much value on storytelling. As a result, we not only lose a valuable method of communication and learning, but we lose a lot of humor.

The best way to hold onto your funny life stories and those of your close friends and relatives is to write them down. Having a written collection of your own personal humor is a really effective way to combat stress with humor. One glance at the stories in your collection will demonstrate that they almost always deal with situations that were embarrassing or "not funny" when they happened, but they now are among your most treasured and humorous memories.

You will note that I have scattered a number of my own personal funny stories throughout this book. On the next page, you'll find another one, an embarrassing moment from my adolescence.

Brace yourself

When I was a teen, I had braces and contact lenses. This was so long ago that braces were made out of steel, not plastic, and contact lenses were clear. It is important to the story for you to understand that without my contact lenses, I can't see past my nose.

One day, I dropped a contact lens on the white shag carpet at home. I didn't have the other one in, so I got down on my hands and knees to try to find the missing lens. I got down so close to the carpet, in fact, that my braces got stuck in the shag rug. I could hear my dad's voice in my head, "You break those braces and you're grounded for life!" I wasn't even going to try to free myself.

Unfortunately, no one was home. So for the next twenty minutes (although it seemed an eternity), I had to lay face down in the carpet waiting to be rescued. Finally, my stepmother came home and cut me out with a pair of scissors.

The next day at school, I found a stray carpet strand in my braces!

Here are some easy steps for developing your own collection of funny stories:

- Every time something funny happens to you from here on, write it down.

- Try to write down all the funny things that have happened during your life.

- Ask your parents or siblings to tell you funny things they remember and, of course, record them.

- Make it a practice to tell people funny stories. Actually retelling funny stories about yourself is one of the most effective ways of using humor in presentations and speeches—it humanizes you as a speaker and lets you use humor that is completely nonthreatening to the audience because it pokes fun at you, not them!

- Encourage everyone to tell funny stories at family gatherings.

Be prepared
for emergencies

We all have emergencies. Crises. Stressors. Events that, while they're happening, take all our energy just to suffer through them without making rash decisions that will come back to haunt us later.

You've probably heard of the Ten Second Rule— "Almost every crisis can wait ten seconds for you to respond. So, every time a crisis arises, take a deep breath, count slowly to ten, and try to relax. Then respond calmly to the crisis."

Now think how much better the Ten Second Rule would be if you could actually laugh during those ten seconds and therefore get the physiological and emotional benefits of laughter, as well as enhancing your problem-solving skills. Those ten seconds would be really worthwhile.

In order to find the laughter during the crisis, you have to prepare beforehand. These days, a lot of our bad news comes over the phone or is recorded on voicemail or on an answering machine). This allows you many alternatives that you don't necessarily have when dealing with bad news face-to-face.

Prepare for these situations by making a list of humor options that you think would work for you. You might consider some of these ideas:

■ Make faces.

- Roll over and play dead on the floor.

- Make loud noises with your armpit.

- Press a noisemaker.

- Pretend you're strangling yourself with the phone cord.

- Make gagging motions.

- Line all your troll dolls up and have a troll war in which your side wins because of superior intellect and skill.

- Doodle ugly pictures of the person delivering bad news.

Start your own humor stress relief kit. You know how important a first aid kit is in physical emergencies? Well, a humor relief kit can serve that same role when your psyche needs a Band-Aid.

Include in your kit anything guaranteed to make you laugh. This includes stuff you've bought (see "Spend Your Money on Funny"), as well as cartoons, newspaper headlines, typos in letters, funny pictures, inadvertent humor, one-liners from *The Tonight Show* . . . whatever. It doesn't have to make anyone else laugh—just you.

Collect all these things in a place where you can have ready access to them during emergencies—whether that's a file drawer, a shoebox, your glove box, your briefcase, or whatever. Better yet, just buy yourself a funny toy box meant for children and tuck your humor relief kit materials inside.

Adopt
an alias

We all have sides to our personalities that aren't always pleasant. Even if you try to start seeing the funny side of things more often, there will be frequent occasions when the "evil you" will win and the "good you" will end up locked in a closet somewhere. This is particularly true during situations that are known to set you off.

One great way to try to deal with the "evil you" is to

give him or her a name. Let's say you choose the name "Helga," for example. If you are ranting and raving about a certain situation and then realize you could be reaching out for humor, all you have to do is say, "How did Helga get here? I thought I left her at home!"

Giving a name to your not-so-pleasant side also makes it easier to receive criticism. If, for example, your spouse criticizes your behavior, but actually calls you Helga instead of your real name, you and your spouse both get a little more levity out of the moment. And you have a chance to realize that perhaps it is time for Helga to go home for a while.

If you are in a long-term relationship, of course, this process of naming your bad side goes both ways.

You can laugh if you want to

A wide number of studies have shown that you don't have to feel like laughing to get the physiological and emotional benefits of laughter. Ask yourself this question: Have you ever exercised when you didn't feel like it, and did you get the benefits of exercising anyway?

It's the same with laughter. So follow these guidelines:

- Set a "laugh out loud" daily goal for yourself.

  Evaluate how often you already laugh out loud and

set your first goal 20 percent higher. Your goal is to laugh out loud because there are more physiological benefits from laughing out loud than from simply smiling or feeling happy.

■ Simply sit at your desk or in your car or at home on the couch and laugh. You don't have to have a reason. This is exercise. And it's certainly more fun than sit-ups!

■ Tell anyone who questions your behavior that it is a new exercise program guaranteed to improve health and happiness—and you don't even have to wear a leotard or running shoes.

What you would have learned if you hadn't skipped this chapter

- Funny friends can make your life healthier and happier.

- Maybe you can't buy happiness, but you can buy things that make you laugh.

- You can develop your own humor library.

- Communicating with humor is fun and effective.

- You should try to remember funny things that happen to you.

- You should prepare emergency humor response options.

- It's easier to laugh at yourself if you go by an alias.

- You don't have to feel like laughing to get the benefits of laughter.

Humor tools: advanced lessons

Comedians are experts at turning life's little tragedies into comedy. Since that is ultimately what you want to be able to do in order to lead a less stressful, more fun-filled life, let's look at some of the tricks of the trade.

Joke formulas

Seeing the jokes life plays on you is made easier if you look at some of the primary joke formulas that comedians use to think and write humorously. Without being aware of it, you probably use most of these formulas in what you say and write every day, but actually applying them to your stressors will give you a structure to rely upon when you need to find the funny in life.

The formulas:

- Comparison—Compare something to something out-of-the ordinary or just comedic in nature.

  Example: "I'm so agitated I could wash a load of laundry in my sleep."

- Definition—Redefine a word comedically.

  Example: "Stress—what happens when your brain says no and your mouth says, 'Of course, I'd be glad to.'"

- Exaggeration—Blow something up out of proportion.

  Example: "I'm under so much stress that when I went to yoga class I got stuck in the lotus position and they had to call the paramedics to pry me loose with the jaws of life!"

- Lists—Phrases or words on a theme, some or all of which are   funny (you probably are familiar with David Letterman's Top-Ten Lists.)

  Example: Top Seven Ways to Lose Ten Pounds Overnight

  7. Remove your ten-pound ankle weights before going to bed.

6. Shave your head (this assumes you have lots of heavy hair).

5. Donate a 10-pound bag of sugar to a food pantry.

4. Move somewhere with less gravity.

3. Donate a few major organs.

2. Remove your cat from his sleeping spot on your face.

1. Give birth.

■ Observation—Look at an everyday occurrence in a comedic way (these are the types of jokes Jerry Seinfeld is famous for).

Example: "Why do they call them connecting flights? They're usually at opposite ends of the airport."

Comedians use many other joke formulas, but these are the easiest, the types you are probably already using without knowing it, and the most applicable to stress management.

As an exercise to convince yourself how easy it can be to take your stressors and write something funny about them, write down something that is causing you stress, for example: I'm broke and the rent is due. Then write a list of funny ways to solve the problem, for example, rent out your apartment for bingo games, have a cat wash, auction off your roommate's belongings . . .

These joke formulas will be useful to you as you try some of the rest of the exercises in this chapter.

Brainstorming to find the funny

Finding the funny in your daily stressors requires that you do some work—after all, if responding to negative situations with the fight or flight syndrome is "natural," you have to put some effort into choosing a different, but definitely healthier approach to life.

One way that comedians begin to try to find humor in their material (e.g., their stressful lives) is to approach their lives with the basic journalistic questions: who, what, when, where, how, and why. By asking these questions about an issue, they are brainstorming with themselves to find a funnier perspective.

For the sake of this exercise, let's work with a moderate stressor from my life—the fact that I've put on a few pounds recently. Now, before I get worried, overly-concerned, annoyed, or angry, I'll apply the journalistic questions and see where the humor is.

The list on the next page includes some of the things that one might associate with weight gain, weight loss, or dieting:

Who	What	When
Oprah Winfrey	Rabbit food	Before reunion
Richard Simmons	Will power	For big date
Susan Powter	Calorie counting	When pants don't fit
Twiggy	Starvation	During mid-life crisis
Dr. Dean Ornish	Cheating	After the holidays

Where	Why	How
Grocery store	Spouse is on diet	SlimFast
Hospital	No money	Liposuction
Fast food restaurant	Low self-esteem	Appetite suppressants
Jenny Craig Clinic	For their health	Stomach stapling
All you can eat cafe	Doctor's orders	Exercise

These are just a few of the things you might associate with the topic. The next step is to simply state the stressor and try to use the list to find something funny about it. Here are some examples:

- I've really got to lose some weight (statement of stressful situation).

- I've decided to have my stomach velcroed. (This idea came up when looking at stomach stapling in the "How" list.)

- I've heard that calorie counting burns sixty calories an hour.

- If I don't, I'm going to end up having to play Santa Claus at the next holiday party.

- I wonder if Richard Simmons makes housecalls.

- I wonder if the Jenny Craig Clinic has an all you-can-eat buffet.

- I don't understand why my diet's not working. I'm drinking a SlimFast with every meal.

- My self esteem is lower than a dachshund.

If you take the time to "play around" with your stressors until you find something associated with them that tickles your funny bone, you are well on your way to developing a more humorous perspective on life. Remember, the goal is not to write jokes that other people will necessarily find funny—it's to come up with a way of thinking about your situation that will make you laugh.

Keeping a humor diary

Both of the previous exercises gave you some structured ways to start developing your ability to find humor in life. However, unless you regularly apply those techniques, you will, out of habit, fall into the old rut of responding negatively to stressors. That is why a humor diary can be one of the best ways to cope with your stress every day.

Mental health experts have suggested for years that

simply writing down the things that bother you may help you deal with them more effectively. If you are consistent about keeping a diary, you can look back at things you were worried about two months or two years ago and see that the worst didn't happen, or, if it did, how you survived it anyway.

If, in addition to simply writing down your stressors, you can apply the joke formulas and journalistic questions to create humor, you enhance your ability to cope. Here, then, are some tips for making a humor diary work for you:

- Choose a convenient format. If you prefer to keep your diary on a computer, do so. If you prefer pen and paper, choose that. Make sure, however, that you choose a large enough notebook to have plenty of space to write down your stressors, your association lists, and your jokes.

- Apply yourself. Get into the habit of writing something down every day. You may find that in the beginning, writing humor is difficult. Fine. Simply write down your stressors. Then, in a few weeks, when you've had a chance to cool down and let go of some of the misery, return to those stressors and go through the exercises. Pretty soon you should be able find the humor on the day you write down the stressor.

■ In addition to the joke formulas and journalistic questions, one of the simplest ways to try to find some humor in your diary entries is to imagine how someone else might handle the situation. This works especially well if you choose someone who is funny and who you admire.

I often ask myself how "Murphy Brown"—I know she's a fictional character, but I still admire her— would handle my stressors. Her typical responses to crises include: blaming things on someone else, firing her secretaries, throwing darts at pictures of people who cause her trouble, making everyone else miserable so that by comparison she feels better, and playing pranks (such as having pizza delivered at odd hours throughout the night to people who've caused her grief). While I may not choose to respond to my stressors in any of those ways, simply writing down these ideas in my humor diary makes me feel better.

- If, in the course of your day, you actually find some humor in your mini-tragedies, use your diary to record what it was that you found funny. Did someone tell you a funny story about a similar situation? Did you cope by saying something funny? Did you force yourself to laugh? This will provide you a regular reminder of the types of things that work to help you move from anger to laughter.

- Ask yourself as you write down the negative parts of your day, "What would have made it worse?" Sometimes, simply imagining a worse scenario can help you put your situation in perspective and find the humor in it. Take a simple situation like spilling coffee on your pants at an important meeting. How could that be worse? Well, you could have spilled coffee on the company president's pants. Now you have an improved, and humorous, perspective on the situation.

- Also include in your humor diary anything funny that happened during the day whether or not it was associated with a stressor. If you are keeping a paper diary, you can actually tape things like cartoons and funny letters in your notebook.

Remember, you are keeping a diary for your own physical and mental well-being. Don't worry about whether something is funny to someone else. Remember what Steve Allen, Jr., says, "If it's funny to you, it's funny!"

Humor personal ads

If you are trying to find the humorous person inside you, perhaps what you need is—a personal ad.

Here's the plan. Get out a pen or keyboard and compose your own personal ad. Describe the "you" that is stressed out—the one who's overworked; the one with a full professional calendar, but no social calendar; the one who thinks fun is something people who aren't serious about their jobs have on the weekend.

Now, describe the happy, joyful, funny you—the you that you'd like to get in touch with more often. Here are some sample personal ads to help you with this exercise:

Wanted: playmate

Overworked, overstressed person seeking inner child with whom I can go out to play. My hobbies include saying "yes," worrying about stuff that never happens, and juggling. Guilt is my middle name. My play companion must be able to lie in the grass watching clouds go by, make sand castles, fly a kite, play with animals, and color outside the lines!

Wanted: someone to take care of me

Workaholic perfectionist. My hobbies include trying to please everyone and self-criticism. I am too short/tall, too skinny/fat, and have had a bad hair life. Looking for someone who is kind and caring, who pays attention to my needs, who will look at me and say, "You look mahvelous—you are mahvelous!"

Wanted: assertive, supportive companion

Manic mother of many seeks someone who can teach me to stand up and say, "Enough already!" Looking for someone to share quiet evenings watching movies that don't feature Barney or Power Rangers; listening to music that doesn't make my hair stand on end; not worrying about homework or school brownies or whether any of my children is getting another body part pierced!

This can be a simple, yet effective, way to remind yourself to stop and smell the funny in life!

Writing a humor resume

You have a resume, right? And as entertaining reading it rates two thumbs down, right? Well, who says all you are and all you have to offer the world can be stuck in categories such as educational experience, previous jobs, and references?

As you get more in touch with your humorous side, writing a humor resume can help remind you that you are a multifaceted person and that what you do for an "occupation" is just that—something to keep you occupied. A humor resume helps you stay in touch with the real—and playful—you.

Here are some ideas for what to include on your resume:

- Funny skills or talents: Can you juggle, mime, clown, bellydance, hula-hoop, do impressions of all your relatives, sing off-key, make up silly commercial jingles, write limericks, draw humorous stick figures, or just plain make people laugh? Make a list of all your unique skills and talents and, if it's not very long, check out your local community college calendar for classes that look like fun!

- **Bad/funny habits:** Bad habits can be annoying, but they can also be funny. My husband is a born klutz and this has proven to be a wellspring of humor around our house. Do you tend to exaggerate, always correct other people's spelling, never put the lid on the toothpaste, show up late to everything, have a black thumb, never get the laundry in the basket, always require a bottle of White Out to balance your checkbook?

Remember, some of the most effective humor to use in communicating with others is to poke fun at yourself! When I speak, I often note how I tend to spit when I talk fast. I say, "It doesn't bother me, but often the people in the front row send me their drycleaning bills."

- **Unusual interests or hobbies:** I myself speed-crochet. I once made an entire afghan in three days. (And who says, crocheting is relaxing?) Do you collect Elvis memoribilia, analyze other people's handwriting, bungee jump, swim in iced-over lakes, color, blow bubbles, perform karaoke, grow ragweed, or have some other fascinating hobby?

- **Unusual jobs you've had:** One man I met during a workshop has spent his entire life working at odd jobs close to Disney attractions with the hope of eventually becoming a Disney character. If you include jobs from early in your childhood, you're bound to come up with some that are interesting and unusual. I myself have spray-painted street numbers on curbs (with a partner who kept missing the curb and spraying my arms), sold chili door-to-door, and worked for a eccentric multi-millionaire who used to take mid-afternoon naps on the middle of his office floor.

■ As long as you're at it, you can take the typical
resume categories and use them humorously. I
always tell people I have a B.S. in B.S. My M.P.H.,
which actually stands for Masters of Public Health,
I call a "Might Possibly be Humorous" degree. I
blame all my shortcomings on the fact that I didn't
go to kindergarten. You, too, can find humor in
your school, your degrees, and your references.

Your humor resume is a great way to remind yourself
of your own humor skills—skills you should call upon
when you're feeling overstressed or blue. Be sure to continue to update your resume as you build up your reper-
toire of humor skills and funny preoccupations.

Rewriting
your
autobiography

When I teach comedy writing and performance, we always start by writing a 3–5 page autobiography, focusing
on the life issues that have had the biggest impact on each
student's life. Throughout the course of the class, that
autobiography serves as the material for the students'
stand-up routines.

The reason I use this method is that it not only
provides material about which the students have strong
emotions (and emotion is very important to effective
comedy), but it actually provides a therapeutic effect. I

have had students deal with abuse, alcoholism, loss, grief, and even rape in this manner.

When it comes to your own personal history, it is important to remember that there is no "reality." Everything from the past is perception. And as with your daily stressors, you can choose to perceive your past stressors in a positive, or humorous light.

Here are a few examples from my humor autobiography:

■ I had so many step- and half-siblings, we had to wear nametags to the dinner table so we could know who to yell at for taking the last roll.

■ Our family's love was expressed in a variety of ways, including not referring to the step-siblings as "the spawn of Satan."

■ My third stepmother had an interesting hobby - attempted suicide. She slit her wrists so many times her arms were six inches shorter than the day she married my dad.

In each of the above "jokes" the first sentence is "truth." Everything after that is the humor spin. My basic philosophy is that you can choose to be miserable about your past, point your finger and blame your entire rotten life on your parents, siblings, or people who picked on you in school, etc. We all have dysfunctional pasts that contribute to our current misery. Or you can, as The Eagles say, "Get over it." Humor helps you put your past life in perspective.

"Change is good" mantra

- I am a flexible person who welcomes and celebrates change.

- I embrace the change of seasons. I am comfortable with changing my opinion. Over the years, my taste in music has changed and that is good.

- I look forward at the end of every day to changing my underwear.

- I appreciate the changing scenery when on a long trip. I have been known to change out of sweats and tennis shoes into something a little dressier for formal occasions. I often change my mind, even without realizing it. I know how many lawyers it takes to change a lightbulb.

- I encourage other people to change so they will better meet my expectations of what is right and good. I frequently use the remote control to change the channels. I love going to a fast food restaurant and getting back change.

- I am a flexible person who welcomes and celebrates change.

Using the skills you have learned in the earlier parts of this chapter, you can write your own humor autobiography. It could be one of the best ways to deal with your old baggage and move forward to a life full of laughter and joy. It certainly worked for me.

Using top ten lists to problem-solve

Rather than letting simple stressors erupt into major issues, you can use your humor skills to defuse them early.

Imagine, for example, that you are having a running disagreement with people in your office over the best way to deal with a decreased budget. You have your ideas and they has theirs, and it seems as if never the twain shall meet.

By sitting down together to come up with funny solutions in the form of a top ten list, you will accomplish a number of things. First, you will get your creative juices flowing, which will, in turn, allow you to think more clearly about real possible solutions. Second, you will change your perspective, which will allow you to step back from your opinion and perhaps get a better idea of what the other people are saying. Third, by laughing together, you will find it easier to work with the people with whom you've been feuding. And, who knows, one of your funny solutions may actually work!

Here is a sample top ten list of funny ways to raise money for your company:

10. Have the company president go on *Wheel of Fortune*.

9. Build a dunking booth and put the least popular company manager in it.

8. Borrow money from your competitor.

7. Enter the Publisher's Clearinghouse Sweepstakes.

6. Write a country and western song.

5. Charge admission to visitors.

4. Auction off company secrets to the highest bidder.

3. Start a 1-900 Psychic Hotline in the secretarial pool.

2. Make a videotape of a day in the life of the office and send it to *America's Funniest Videos*.

1. Hold bingo games in the company headquarters on weekends.

What you would have learned if you hadn't skipped this chapter

- Some simple structured tools can help you put more laughter in your life.

- Moving from anger to humor often requires hard work and discipline, but it's very much worth the effort.

Help!
I can't remember
all this stuff!

Refer to the list on the following page to quickly remember the steps for replacing the stress in your life with laughter.

HOLD ON! I'M NOT FINISHED YET!!

A final note from the author

It's worth repeating, "Don't Get Mad, Get Funny." In fact, write it down and put it in plain sight (how about taping it to your forehead). Good luck and good laughter.

Additional resources on the positive benefits of laughter

Books

■ Flavier, J.M. "The lessons of laughter." World Health Forum, 11(4):412–15, 1990.

■ Fry, W. "Humor and the human cardiovascular system." In: Mindess, H., and J. Turek (editors). The Study of Humor. Los Angeles: Antioch University, 1979.

■ Fry, W.F. and M. Savin. "Mirthful laughter and blood pressure." Humor, 1:49–62, 1988.

- Fry, W.F. "The physiologic effects of humor, mirth, and laughter." *Journal of the American Medical Association*, 267(13):1857–58, 1992.

- Goldstein, J.H. "Therapeutic effects of humor." In: Fry, W.F. and W.A. Salameh. Handbook of Humor and Psychotherapy: Advances in the Clinical Use of Humor. Sarasota, Florida: Professional Resource: Jeremy Tarcher, Inc., 1989.

- Klein, A. "The Healing Power of Humor." Los Angeles. *Journal Biological Psychology*, 19:39–50, 1977.

- Robinson, V.M. *Humor and the Health Professions: The Therapeutic Use of Humor in Health Care.* Thorofare, New Jersey: SLACK Incorporated, 1991.

Catalogs featuring funny products

- Brainstorms, 1-800-231-6000

- Humor Resources, 1-518-587-8770

- Moose School Productions, 1-800-676-5480

- Oriental Trading, 1-800-228-2269

- Stress Queens, Inc., 1-800-262-7494

- Wireless, 1-800-669-9999

OTHER SELF-HELP BOOKS
FROM WHOLE PERSON ASSOCIATES

KICKING YOUR STRESS HABITS:
A Do-It-Yourself Guide for Coping with Stress
Donald A. Tubesing, PhD

Over a quarter of a million people have found ways to deal with their everyday stress by using **Kicking Your Stress Habits**. This workshop-in-a-book actively involves the reader in assessing stressful patterns and developing more effective coping strategies with helpful "Stop and Reflect" sections in each chapter.

❏ **Kicking Your Stress Habits / $14.95**

SEEKING YOUR HEALTHY BALANCE:
A Do-It-Yourself Guide to Whole Person Well-Being
Donald A. Tubesing, PhD and Nancy Loving Tubesing, EdD

Where can people find the time and energy to "do it all" without sacrificing health and well-being? **Seeking Your Healthy Balance** helps readers discover how to develop a more balanced lifestyle by learning effective ways to juggle work, self, and others; by clarifying self-care options; and by discovering and setting their own personal priorities.

Seeking Your Healthy Balance asks the questions that help readers find their own answers.

❏ **Seeking Your Healthy Balance / $14.95**

For more information, to receive our current catalog, or to order, call toll free (800) 247-6789.